AF585527

Wakefield Press

Hair and There

Born and raised in Adelaide, Heather Caddick has had a diverse career spanning kindergarten teaching to stockbroking and investment. She is passionate about voluntary work encompassing wildlife and humanitarian causes. When not travelling she lives in Adelaide with her husband Alfie. This is her fifth book.

By the same author

For the Love of Rhinos

The Road Less Travelled

This Life in Rhymes and Riddles

Flying with Cranes

Hair and There
(a world of blowdries)

Heather Caddick

Wakefield Press

Wakefield Press
16 Rose Street
Mile End
South Australia 5031
www.wakefieldpress.com.au

First published 2022

Copyright © Heather Caddick, 2022

All rights reserved. This book is copyright. Apart from any fair dealing for the purposes of private study, research, criticism or review, as permitted under the Copyright Act, no part may be reproduced without written permission. Enquiries should be addressed to the publisher.

Edited by Julia Beaven, Wakefield Press
Design by Liz Nicholson, Wakefield Press
Typeset by Michael Deves, Wakefield Press

ISBN 978 1 74305 963 0

A catalogue record for this book is available from the National Library of Australia

Wakefield Press thanks Coriole Vineyards for continued support

For Tilda, Emmy, Natalia and Annabel

Contents

Namibia, 2018

Behind almost every woman stands a man
who has let her down.

NAOMI BLIVEN

Windhoek, Namibia's capital, is small, Germanic and charming, with a beautiful park nestling in the city's heart. Races combine here, with Kalahari Bushmen (the San peoples), southern Black Africans, and white descendants of the once German Colony. The mix works with a conservative regime, supported by a strong majority of its people.

A shopping mall leads to an arcade, where in a corner booth lies 'Inge's Hairstyles'. I have been coming to Inge for years, and she greets me like an old friend with Mara her African offsider rushing over to say hello.

Mara is huge in stature and spirit, with an infectious laugh that fills the room as she greets me, a towel over one shoulder, and wearing a voluminous apron. She leads me to the washbasin and begins to shampoo my hair, talking and laughing as she massages my scalp, before she leads me back to Inge.

Inge has weathered the storm of life well. She married young to a Germanic, good-looking but feckless individual, back when white women did not work in this community. So she stayed home to care for husband and children, within the arms of the Lutheran church. The husband wandered off and left her to fend for herself and bring up their three children alone. The church

helped a little, and she started working as a hairdresser's assistant to bring in some money.

Learning the tricks of the trade and gaining stature, she progressed to become a qualified hairdresser. Ten years ago she opened her corner booth. It is now a thriving business.

Her children have all been schooled, and are working in Namibia and South Africa.

Inge is lined and weathered but with bright twinkling eyes and an alert interest in everything around her, transforming her face. A passionate Namibian, she applauds the government for dividing this enormous country into communal conservancies, which has empowered the different regions to conserve the wildlife and wild habitats, to encourage tourism and the money it brings in, giving pride to the local people.

Every year the best conservancy is named and applauded, receiving an award that is eagerly sought by the whole of Namibia.

We discuss the Kalahari Bushmen, many of whom have traipsed to the city to find work, and are usually rejected.

'It is the young who come here,' she says, 'and it's a huge problem because they live between the skills and rites of their upbringing, and the magnetic temptations of Western city culture.'

Small in stature, wiry and speaking with the clicked tongue, they are a huge problem for the Namibian government. Some have opened stores and eke out a living selling artefacts, but most are on the streets of Windhoek in no-man's-land.

Some of them have found success after working for the tourism industry as Kalahari Bushmen guides, taking tourists

Mother and child, Namibia

On safari with Emmy, Namibia

Making friends with schoolchildren, Namibia

With Alfie at a lion-breeding facility, Namibia

Namibia, sunset

to the Kalahari Desert and the Serengeti, and revealing the intricacies of their traditions and culture.

'Somehow we must fully develop this sector,' she says. 'We must look after our Kalahari people, and this is the best way to do it.'

Inge is excited about meeting her children in Swakopmund, the beautiful seaside resort on the Atlantic coastline. Soon it will be holidays, and they are catching some family time together.

My hair is done, and we say goodbye, with Mara rushing to hug me as I approach the door.

Shiraz, Iran, 2019

Freedom of press and speech, what a blessing for a country in the hands of honest men, what a curse in the hands of demagogues

WILLIAM BOETCKER

Shiraz shimmers in the morning light, a verdant valley of vines bordered by mountains. Everywhere there are shady trees, and water gurgles and flows through aqueducts, leading to pools surrounded by flowers, before flowing on.

We have been gobsmacked by the ancient beauty of mosaicked buildings, arches and architraves, wandering from site to site, slowly taking in the unbelievable sophistication of ancient times.

We stop to rest in a beautiful garden of zinnias and roses, and we are not alone. Local Iranians of all ages and stages are using this garden to meet, to reflect and to pause a while before continuing on.

Scarves are worn by all women, brightly coloured and swathed cleverly, revealing beautiful faces, some with designer sunglasses. Men tend to congregate together and we see chess being played under shady trees.

We are approached by university students who want to practise their English with us, and talk about life outside Iran. Good manners and polite interaction is the way they communicate.

'Change will happen!' a young girl says to me, 'the Mullahs are ageing and life is changing here, and faster than the world realises.'

A hotel garden oasis, Shiraz

Meeting and chatting with students on a dusk promenade in Isfahan

Enjoying a sunset in Shiraz

As we end our conversation, I ask if they know of a hairdresser for me to visit, and I am given a mobile phone to book an appointment at a salon nearby.

I approach a huge wall and a security entrance system, and on stating my appointment, the gate opens and I enter another world. Girls in leggings and midriff tops, no scarves and dark hair swept up into pert ponytails, greet me, and a young man who speaks English ushers me to a chair.

Soon another girl, svelte, midriffed and with rimless glasses mirroring flashing eyes, approaches and, in faltering English, establishes what I would like. takes me to the shampooing arena, where leather massage chairs circle a central washing area.

I relax into the chair as it begins to move with a pulsating circular motion. My back muscles relax completely as my hair is washed and towel dried and I take my place under a chandelier, floor-length mirrors lining the wall.

My colouring is unusual here, and one by one each hairdresser comes over to practise their English and to comment on the way I look, which is an amazing boost to the ego of a seventy-year-old!

I am mesmerised by the scarf-swathed women who enter the salon and, once inside the high walls, take off their outer garments to reveal the sexiest outfits with leggings and brief tops, their luxuriant hair cascading around their shoulders, framing perfectly made-up faces.

On leaving they don their outer garments and swathe scarves around their coiffed hair, to emerge into the world as a modest and compliant Iranian woman.

Coffee and 'petit fours' are offered as I wait for my stylist. I love the fun, laughter and gossip and inclusive ambience of this

place. It is a haven for women to spend time here, to catch up with their friends, and to plan their social lives.

My stylist arrives and the blowdry is expertly done, with a circle of admirers around him, watching his every move.

I am asked to comment in English about my experience in the salon on Facebook, and happily do so. It seems there are foreign Facebook followers who click on this site, and the publicity will be good for their business.

Finally I swathe my scarf over the newly coiffed hair and say my goodbyes to them all.

This has been my 'lifting the veil' experience in Iran, and has restored my belief in a slow and quiet movement of denial and freedom. It augurs well for the future of this beautiful and fascinating country.

Paris, 2020

Individuality is everywhere, to be respected as the foundation of everything good

JEAN PAUL RICHTER

I am in Paris alone. It is heaven to walk the streets and breathe in the atmosphere, the smell of cinnamon wafting from a nearby bakery, the perfect fruit and vegetables being stacked on a pavement stand nearby among the rush and bustle of Parisians, chic and superbly dressed in overcoats with scarves tied just so.

My tiny hotel lies in Rue de Bourgogne, around the corner from Musee Rodin. It has a small courtyard lined with flowering shrubs, and an antique bell dangles over the entrance.

Reception is in the hallway, with a dining room for eight people adjacent. I can smell warm croissants and exquisitely brewed coffee wafting from the kitchen.

The lift barely has space for one person let alone a suitcase, so I ascend to my room by lift, with my case being carried up the stairs by the porter. My room has a large window overlooking the courtyard, and the bed fills the room with a tiny chair squeezed into a corner space, and one large cupboard for clothes.

It is just perfect. I go downstairs to the dining room for a late breakfast.

Nina from Tangiers, the cook and waitress, is larger than life with a generous smile and hearty laugh. She speaks no English, so my French needs to make do.

'Je voudrais croissant avec miel, et cafe au lait, s'il vous plâit' prompts a tirade of French from her. I hope my reply of *oui oui* does not reveal my lack of understanding.

Nina pours the coffee and brings warm croissants with honey and jams to complete the breakfast. It tastes like heaven on earth.

I am ready to walk the streets of Paris, but feel decidedly non-chic. I really need to upgrade a little, to Parisian standards, so I stop by a hairdresser who is just opening his doors.

Pascal is tall and graceful with a shock of grey hair coiffed to perfection, and the sides cut short. He wears a silk smock and sashays around his premises with flair and purpose. I ask if he is able to fit me in, and he stands close to me and regards me with a concerned look his face. He then stands back and announces, 'Madame, of course, but might I suggest a total change in your appearance! I think you need a bleach rinse, with the cut to accentuate your facial features.'

He turns my face to one side, regards the profile and then gently moves my face to the other side to contemplate the task ahead.

I agree and am swathed in a grey silk smock and guided to the washing arena where the bleach rinse is rubbed into my scalp, and the hair ruffled. I sit obediently for five minutes before the bleach rinse is washed away.

As Pascal cuts and shapes my hair, he tells me his boyfriend is an artist and works for a framing business nearby. They are from the Provinces and just love being in Paris, where they are able to live the lives they want with all that Paris has to offer.

The trim is becoming a major cut and I look rather intimidated as Pascal reaches for the hair drier. He swirls and straightens,

curls and turns the apparatus with skill, and I see a new me emerging in the mirror. At last it is done, and as I am about to depart Pascal says, 'Let's go for a coffee next door, and I can show off my latest hairstyle.'

We go to Cafe la Grenouille and order. The owner and his friends gather making admiring comments. We settle to superb lattes and petit fours chatting and exchanging views on myriad topics, before Pascal needs to return to work.

I now have a firm friend in Rue de Bourgogne, and emerge from La Grenouille ready to explore the wonders of Paris.

Paris – *'C'est magnifique!'*

Ethiopia, 1994

In a free country there is much clamour with little suffering; in a despotic state there is little complaint but much suffering

HIPPOLYTE CARNOT

I am in Ethiopia with an international group from UNICEF to assess the damage from war and famine, and to visit remote areas where we sent funding after the Live Aid appeal.

I arrive in Addis Ababa to a slew of security checks and a vigorous body search by a female official. I giggle with her as she conducts the operation, which instantly dissolves the tension, and finally I am released to the chaos of Addis.

The road to the city has a median strip littered with the homeless who have travelled from rural areas to a city with nowhere for them to stay.. Mainly ex-army, they are dishevelled and in no-man's-land. Makeshift beds and possessions lie under trees that offer shade from a hot and dry day. Pop-up market stalls sell food, and life in Addis continues on around them, despite this influx of refugees.

We turn into a lane that leads to the hotel, a shabby building, but regarded by UNICEF as secure and well-run. My car drives to a back entrance, where I am welcomed by the owner.

This hotel is run by a family that have just managed to scrape out a living during the upheavals and horrors of Mengistu's Red Terror regime. That era is now over, and the turbulence

is subsiding to a more normal way of life under the new government.

Almaz (diamond in Amharic) shows me to my room, a room that has seen better days. There is an en-suite bathroom, but there is a problem with the water supply in Addis. Infrastructure here has been on its knees since the war, so I am only allowed to use the shower between 7 am and 8 am.

A window in the bedroom allows views to the hotel's garden, but beyond some fields is the airport runway, which explodes with sound every few minutes as aircraft take off and land.

I have a free day until I meet with UNICEF colleagues, and so I go downstairs to the restaurant, where I seem to be the only non-Ethiopian present. Immediately I am engulfed by people concerned I am being cared for, and offering to help me.

Over coffee and an omelette (the extent of the menu) I find someone who will take me to the Mercato, the largest market in Africa.

Ebo is an employee at the hotel and we take a hotel car for the drive to the other side of Addis and park in a quiet lane. He escorts me through myriad stores exhibiting everything from Ethiopian artefacts and Christian symbols to clothing, household items and food.

I am walking ahead of Ebo to see the ornate umbrellas on sale. Priests use these for their ceremonies. Suddenly I feel a twitch at my neck and the tiny gold chain I wear has been ripped off, and the child who has done so is running hell for leather down the street. Ebo quickly comes to my side with a drawn knife ready to protect me, but all is quiet and I hope the assailant makes the most of his windfall.

The poverty in Addis is tangible, and the Mercato is a perfect place for the desperate to try their luck. We gather our thoughts and slowly wander back to the car.

Driving back to the hotel, we share the road with donkeys pulling carts, motor scooters and foul mini bus exhaust fumes that puff out in large gusts as passengers are picked up and delivered at the kerbside.

I decide on a quiet visit to a hairdresser close to the hotel, a contrast to the morning's dramas. Ebo stops the car and I enter the salon.

I am greeted with surprise. This salon specialises in braiding, and I can see a beautiful Ethiopian girl being attended to. The process usually takes three hours, as each hair is segregated and plaited in fine lines across the scalp. The braiding is a magnificent complement to a classically beautiful Ethiopian face, and this girl's high cheekbones and stunning profile make a glamorous result.

I ask for a simple blowdry. Liya, the hair stylist, guides me to a basin, where a bucket of water stands, and she sluices my hair from the bucket before applying shampoo.

'We need to conserve water,' she says. 'They promise to restore the normal supply soon.' She raises her eyebrows with cynicism and adds,

'God knows when that will be!'

Liya speaks good English learnt from her father who worked at the British Embassy as the ambassador's driver. She lost her boyfriend in the war and has not married.

'I am happy,' she says. 'The war is past and we look to the future. My business and my clients are everything to me and the church provides a great social life.'

This is made abundantly clear that night, as a church congregation near the hotel rings out with music, laughter and good cheer for hours after my bedtime.

I return to my hotel with a deeper understanding of the current state of play in Addis, and look forward to visiting the regions over the next two weeks.

Bursa, Turkey, 1992

Experience has convinced me that there is a thousand
times more goodness, wisdom and love
in the world than we imagine

GEHLES

We are in Bursa *en famille*, taking a cheap and cheerful holiday in Turkey and staying in Bursa before venturing up the mountain to ski in Uludag.

Bursa was the original capital of the Ottoman Empire and Mount Uludag towers above the city. During Roman times the elite would spend their summers here, diverting to Uludag to escape the heat.

The ancient forests and undulating hills create a luscious border to this ancient city. Bursa is famous for its thermal springs, and bathhouses have been in existence here for centuries.

We are staying in a tiny hotel on the hillside with a mosque next door. Our room overlooks a minaret and has a spiral staircase down to the dining room. Further steps lead down to the basement bathhouse, where gushing hot and sulphuric water comes out of the aqueduct into marble baths.

The baths are extraordinary, long and deep, enabling those on a health cure to languish for hours in the healing waters.

We decide to try the baths and the soporific effect of heat and cleansing has an instant effect. It's time for an early night. Just as well, for there is no sleeping in. At 5 am there is a call to

prayer from the mosque outside our window. It is so loud and compelling we all wake in shock, and even closing the window makes no difference. Finally it is over and we realise that this is part of life in Turkey.

Stumbling down to breakfast we're greeted by Lalam and Ahmet, who own the hotel. They are hugely hospitable but speak no English. We make do with gestures until I discover they speak German, so we are fine, and sit down to a classic Turkish breakfast of pita bread, white cheese and olives with the most delicious coffee ever.

It is Turkish coffee, served in espresso cups. We add sugar and stir and taste the aromatic flavour, then chew into a Turkish delight, plump with a walnut in the centre.

Lalam prepares breakfast every day. The Turkish delight is her own concoction, made with roses to scent the glutinous mixture and then studded with swollen walnuts that have been soaking in the rose juice.

She fusses over our boys to see they are eating well, and advises us to visit Bursa's silk market that dates back centuries, being the final destination of the Silk Road from China.

We walk our way to the market through bustling lanes where every form of life can be seen. There are children taking trays of tea to customers, women shopping, men carrying huge parcels to be delivered by hand down lanes too narrow for cars.

Finally we arrive at the Silk Market. It has a large square, around which are the shops selling the finest silks in the world. Turks perfected the manufacture of silk cloth centuries ago, and it became the distribution point for Europe. Most of their finest work goes to Paris.

We pass a hairdresser near the bazaar, and I send my boys along to explore its delights, while I spend time in the salon. Serap greets me in Turkish, and I say, '*Kein Türkei sprache, aber Deutsch?*'

She replies in German, and it amazes me that so many Turks speak German. In the 1990s it was their second language (today their second language is English).

I am brought tea and Turkish delight as I wait for a stylist. The salon is full of women of all ages, and because of my colouring I am an item of interest, answering a barrage of questions from all quarters: where do I come from, how old am I, do I have children? They are genuinely interested and very concerned to know if I am enjoying Bursa.

Afet, my stylist, completes a gorgeous blowdry and, rugging up, I meet my boys returning from the bazaar.

It is intensely cold. Snow is beginning to fall as we make our way back to the hotel, to enjoy another night and early minaret wake-up call, before proceeding to Uludag.

Sighisoara, Romania, 2019

Man is a history-making creature, who can neither repeat his past, nor leave it behind

W.H. AUDEN

We are beguiled by stories of Dracula, as turreted castles and dense forests signal our entry to Sighisoara, in the Transylvanian region of Romania.

The town was built on a Roman fort in the 12th century, and played a strategic role for centuries at the edge of Central Europe.

German artisans and craftsmen dominated the economy and built fortifications to protect the city. There were fifteen guilds in the 17th century, and from these guilds the handcraft artisans spread themselves into small businesses, scattered around the town.

This fortified city is intact, surrounded by a wall with a citadel that sits triumphantly on a hill overlooking the Târnava Mare river. Winding cobbled streets curve their way around the citadel, its heavy stone arches and spiral stairways leading to the fort's lookouts. An enormous clock dominates the central square, and from the clock tower you can see the town spread out below.

We take a horse-drawn cart to see the citadel and surrounding by-ways, and are instantly transported back to ancient times, as the horse clops along the cobbled streets. Our driver is in traditional dress, wearing lederhosen and embroidered shirt with

Sighisoara, the birthplace of Dracula

A Romanian Orthodox seminary, Bucharest

a felt hat. He stops to greet his friends along the way, allowing the horse a rest. With a lurch, we are off again, this time descending from the citadel through narrow lanes shrouded by trees, and coming to a square lined with market stalls.

We farewell our driver and dismount, happy to wander around the market. Stopping to take a coffee we watch the passing parade. It is mainly backpackers and tourists admiring the embroidery and hand-crafted souvenirs. The atmosphere is surreal, it's as if we have been transported back centuries, living in the time of horse-drawn carts and artisan guilds producing exquisite products in and around the citadel.

I choose a scarf beautifully embroidered with the finest threads of silk, before we wander down the hill, passing small shops and cafes, set into the steep slope, with jagged steps leading up to their place of business.

A hairdresser's salon is perched precariously on the slope. I decide to investigate and walk up the stairway to be greeted by Daria. Daria is short, buxom and blonde. I learn later that her background is Hungarian, and her family decided to stay in Transylvania when it was handed over to the Kingdom of Romanian in 1918. Since then they have weathered the storm of communism, and the horrifying Ceauşescu regime.

In many ways Sighisoara remained in its time warp during this time, but now with the gates open to all of Europe, and a steady stream of tourists visiting, life is busy and exciting for Daria.

She ushers me to a washbasin and shampoos my hair with a divine lavender-smelling lather. There are two others in a state of disrepair. She towels me dry, asking me to wait as she attends to them.

I am facing the cliff edge that overlooks the magnificent curve of Târnava Mare river, the city spread out below us. Gentle music plays and I am offered coffee and fudge, before Daria blowdries my hair.

It is a pleasant interlude and I walk down the jagged steps revived and ready to explore more of Sighisoara, sporting a rather bouffant hairdo, sprayed into shape Transylvanian style.

Czech Republic, 1995

I like the dreams of the future better than
the history of the past

THOMAS JEFFERSON

The bloodless Velvet Revolution of 1989 led to the end of the Communist Party of Czechoslovakia. In 1993 it was split into the Czech Republic and Slovakia, becoming a parliamentary democracy.

It is 1995, and we are visiting Prague to see the changes and are staying with relatives of Czech friends from Adelaide. They live in a suburb three train stops from the Old Town, and greet us and treats us like members of their family.

They have weathered the boring monotony of communism. Svata is an architect and Ivana a nurse, but with a dacha in the country, they would spend weekends away from the city, immersing themselves in country life, fishing, walking and nurturing their kitchen garden and fruit trees. And, having no children, life was less complicated. In many ways they were able to live below the radar, dodging much of the oppression of communist life.

We are eager to explore, and hop on the train, where we see a marked difference between the old passengers and the young. The old are generally hunched over and still look shell shocked by the changes to their system of life, whereas the young are vibrant and outgoing, their trendy clothes and hairdos in

absolute contrast to their parents, as they welcome the country's new freedoms with open arms.

We alight at Wenceslas Square, dominated by a huge clock, the twelve Apostles walking around the mechanised structure as the clock chimes. People wait before the hour strikes to watch; many then take a coffee nearby for an hour so they can see the automation once more.

Wenceslas Square is cobbled and large, lined with shops and businesses, and there are pop-up stalls selling food and trinkets. It is the centre of commerce in Prague and it was here the Velvet Revolution took place, with thousands of people gathering, silently holding lit candles in a call for change. Soon after the Communist Party fell, and here we are experiencing the beginning of a new era.

What is so noticeable is the way the young are embracing change as they start businesses and ventures. We sense the energy of enterprise and purpose, and everyone seems to be walking quickly.

We pass a church where a young girl is selling tickets to a classical concert, and we pay around $5 a ticket to enter and sit close to the front. Soon three music students armed with violin, viola and cello enter and play exquisite Mozart, the music echoing through the lofty heights of the church as it takes us to another world, before we re-emerge to the bustle of life outside.

At every turn there is a pop-up stall, an invitation to a musical event, or tour guides offering a service. They are all young and each one paddles his own canoe, in marked contrast to the years of suppression.

We are attracted to a shop with gentle music playing. Realising

it is a hairdresser, I walk in to be greeted by Adriana, who sports a pert ponytail and bright smile. Time to send my bloke off to explore more of Prague as I request a blowdry.

I'm ushered into a small salon, with one large chair that tilts back to facilitate shampooing, and then forward for the styling in front of a huge mirror.

We begin to talk, and as her German is better than English, *Wir sprechen Deutsch.* She comes from Karlovy Vary (Karlsbad), a spa city since the thirteenth century, with a large German-speaking population. The turmoil of Communism did not really affect this historic enclave in Czechoslovakia too much, as long as you kept your head down, and did not challenge the system.

Her parents still live in Karlovy Vary, but she decided to move to Prague and strike out on her own, opening a small hairdressing salon and working dawn till dusk. She sleeps on the premises.

'I am happy,' she says. 'We are all working together to rebuild a way of life, and I have many friends around the Square. There is such a feeling of progress, and it is wonderful to be part of it all.'

I feel the Czech Republic is in safe hands and a towering example of what can be achieved through silent protest.

Dubai, 1985

Remember when the peacock struts his stuff, he shows his backside to the world

HERVE WIENER

Dubai the enigma, a desert settlement charging forward to become a megalopolis in just 40 years.

Back in the 1980s, I visited Dubai regularly en route to Europe, staying there with a dear friend employed by a British desalination company, 51 per cent owned, of course, by the Emirati.

She lived in a spacious and glamorous townhouse overlooking the Persian Gulf. In a small dwelling at the front, a Goanese national named Lorso lived and helped out in the house and garden.

I asked him to talk about his life.

He left home to eke out a living in a place where he could get work, and chose Dubai. Every two years he would fly home to his family to catch up on life in his village. It seemed a lonely life to me, but he had friends in the Goanese community in Dubai, and met with them often. He seemed happy and content.

A trip to the souk and spice markets was top of the list on each visit, meaning a drive to the creek and taking an *abra* (a tiny open timber boat) across the water to the markets of Dubai.

These markets had been thriving for generations. Divided into sections, the spices and food in one area, and the artefacts

Taking some time out in Dubai

and gold in the other, with a maze of passages and arcades where local people sell their wares. In the Gold Souk was a series of buildings, the windows arrayed with the most staggering selection of gold jewellery.

The flamboyant gold jewellery, crafted to suit the tastes of the local people with fancy filigree and symbols, was not necessarily to Western taste, but there was one shop that sold Western-styled jewellery, made in Italy, and it was very hard to resist a purchase on each visit.

The spice markets were a haven for the senses. We could smell the aromas as we approached the stalls packed with sacks of saffron, cardamon pods, cinnamon, cloves and cumin seeds, to name a few, all on display and ours for the asking. I wandered along these arcades, breathing in the fragrant aromas and often stopping to sit and drink a black sweet tea in a little alcove along the way.

The souks are open at night to make the most of the cooler temperatures, and we ventured there to eat falafel and salad, sitting outside in the balmy night air, with the locals spilling around us, shopping, children playing, many gathering to meet friends and socialise.

The extreme heat means that life's rhythm and pace is very different here, and so early mornings and late nights are busy with activity. The middle of the day is for resting.

I met interesting members of prominent local families, always the men and never the women. My friend had an influential position within the company, and we were feted and entertained sumptuously. Most of these locals were educated in England, and they relished the opportunity to interact with us.

On one trip, when I had our two sons in tow, we went into the desert with Ali to watch him train his falcons, with an entourage, including a guy who brought along live doves for the kill.

We watched as he lifted the leather hood from his falcon and waited until a dove was released. Flying fast and aiming for the throat, the dove was felled in an instant. The falcon then flew back to his master and sat on his arm, to be given a treat, before the hood was placed over his head again.

We rode horses from the Polo Club at dawn, heading across the desert. My horse was not a powerful polo pony but a gentle old mare, and to ride across the sand as the sun was rising remains my most enduring memory of this time in the Emirates. The early rays promising heat cast a pink glow over the sand, and the silence settled us as we rode deeper into the desert dunes.

Eventually we wended our way back to the club house for coffee and breakfast.

There was an enticing salon for hair and beauty nearby, run by Filipinos who specialised in treatments for local women. The local women did not work and were closeted in their family compounds, so to come out for treatments was a top priority. It was normal for them to spend a day having their hair done, facials and massage, resting and taking tea.

I was fascinated by threading, an ancient way to remove facial hair. It involves the twirling of cotton threads over the skin, removing the hair, and acting rather like a lawn mower.

It was obvious to see that this was a club for local women, who were able to talk freely together, and enjoy the company of others. Dubai has a very restricted society for women, and

this was their one outlet to exchange views outside their family compounds.

Now, forty years have passed and this life has gone, being replaced by a whizz-bang world of skyscrapers and super highways, with thousands of expats working here, and Dubai becoming the commerce centre for the Middle East.

But, if you go into the desert, far from the city lights, and watch the moon cast its beams over the sand, the magic returns and those indelible memories I have of old Dubai come back, and will remain with me forever.

Helsinki, 1986

Tomorrow to fresh woods and pastures anew

JOHN MILTON

We board the *Queen Sylvia* in Stockholm. This new ship takes cars and cargo, but also has a wonderful resort-style section for passengers. Our boys are excited to be on a ship and make their way to the designated children's play area, while we settle into our cabin before wandering around the decks.

It is mid winter and dark outside as we slowly emerge from Stockholm to the open sea. We gather the children and go to the dining room for a healthy meal, before retiring to our bunks for an early night.

An enormous crash and a rumbling of brittle sounds startles us into action. It sounds as if we have hit an iceberg! The boys sleep on. Should we wake them?

I grab a gown and go into the passage to find a rather relaxed ship's officer wandering around.

'What was that'? I cry.

He smiles at me benignly. 'Oh,' he says, 'that is the sound of our icebreakers at work. We are sailing through a sea of ice, and they pave the way for us to reach Finland.'

It is a relief to know, but we spend a very noisy night trying to sleep, and head off to breakfast very early next morning.

It is bleak and cold as we emerge from the ship to crusty ice surfaces and trees spangled with icy branches as the sun attempts

to rise over the port of Helsinki. Suddenly it emerges to light everything into a wonderland of winter white.

The sun will only be with us for a short while in this northern mid-winter city, so we decide to take a local bus to anywhere, just to see something of Helsinki, and to mix with local people.

Our bus is heading to Toolo, a suburb that is not too far from the CBD. We clamber aboard, and are regarded with some interest by local people on the bus, as we stumble to register our tickets and joke and laugh in English.

Toolo is an excellent example of Nordic Classicism, but looks rather cold and unwelcoming today shrouded in snow, icicles dangling from verandahs and newly shovelled paths leading up to doorways.

Approaching the town centre, we see that the trendy boutiques and cafes are all closed. We alight and walk our way through the market square to a park, crunching on icy paths and over a small bridge until we get to the Sibelius monument. Imposing it might be, but our boys are unimpressed, so we take a round-about walk back to the town.

Relief! There is a cafe opening its doors, so we rush in to the warmth and order hot chocolates and cakes by gesturing and pointing; we have no Finnish and the owner has absolutely no English. He regards us with astonishment before gently smiling and welcoming us into his cafe.

There is a games room attached with a pool table and a wall of games devices, so I bid my boys farewell as they start playing, and head off down the street to investigate.

A hairdresser is opening her doors, and I enter with hand gestures and slow English asking for a blowdry. Lida replies in

Chilly Helsinki

perfect English, and settles me at the washbasin for a shampoo. She has recently completed a gap year in England, and is slowly progressing with an Environmental Science degree. She hopes to join the faculty of Environmental Sciences at Helsinki University when she graduates.

In the meantime she works as a hairdresser to bring in money and to be in contact with the community, in a totally different environment from her chosen profession.

'I love it,' she says at the washbasin. 'This job allows me to meet with women of all ages and stages of life, and they in turn connect me to their lives and everyday struggles, joys and disappointments. It creates a healthy balance for me, between the reality of day-to-day life and my passion for the state of Finland's environment and what we should do about it.'

She finishes her shampooing and we move chairs to continue. 'Finland has reduced pollution and improved its environmental quality through pioneering approaches like so-called 'green taxes'. We are now focusing on the health impacts of pollution and the management of waste. We have achieved good urban air quality, our lakes are recovering from acidification, and we are improving biodiversity in the forests.'

Her passionate talk continues. 'Our Baltic Sea still suffers from eutrophication, which is the excessive input of nutrients causing reduced light conditions in the water and oxygen depletion on the Baltic Sea floor.

This is actually the area that I want to focus on.'

I am completely blindsided by Lida, and her passion for environmental science. She has made me view Finland in a different light.

Suddenly the door opens and in walks a middle-aged woman shrouded in a fur-lined cape, who shakes off the snow at the door, removes her cape to a stand and greets us both in Finnish.

I can see my time with Lida is over, but my impression of Finland has deepened to an understanding that there are people here trying to return the environment to normality – and that even Finland has been polluted and affected by human mismanagement.

Deep in thought I gather my boys from the games room and we rug up and head to the bus stop for our return to Helsinki.

Norfolk Island, 2021

There is no freedom for the weak

GEORGE MEREDITH

We are in the middle of the COVID-19 pandemic. Our state of South Australia has banned all travel overseas and from time to time state borders are slammed shut, either marooning homecoming travellers or causing cancellations of longed-for holidays.

We have been forbidden to travel to see family and our beloved grandchildren in Europe, and so we decide to travel to Norfolk Island for Christmas.

Situated well into the Pacific, and under the governance of New South Wales, it seems a sensible idea to get us out of the debilitating regime of bureaucratic authority, and the snap decisions that have blighted our lives for the past eighteen months.

We need to be mindful that Norfolk is small and very conscious of being susceptible to possible infection, so with our triple vaccinations and a COVID test prior to boarding, we finally take off for our escape.

Norfolk Island has only 2000 residents and many emanate from the mutiny on the Bounty and Fletcher Christian, who moved camp from Pitcairn Island to Norfolk, escaping the tyranny of Captain Bligh.

There are beautiful Islanders, New Zealanders and Australians

living here, and when you go behind the veil of tourism you notice a strong and rigid patriotism to the island, and its place in history.

The ruins of the appalling penal settlement, lining the shores of Emily Bay, is a grim reminder of man's inhumanity to man. A graveyard close to the penal settlement is a permanent testimony to these times. Local people will never venture there at night because ghosts and spirits hover over the graves and unsettling incidents occur if you do so.

The graves are tended and covered with fresh flowers, perhaps for the tourists, but the presence of this graveyard dominates the peace and beauty of this place, lined with Norfolk pine trees, and overlooking the sea.

Wandering cattle have right of way and saunter along the winding roads, oblivious to the pace of life around them. Small cars and miniature trucks use these narrow roads; there is no place for large 4-wheel-drive vehicles here. The shopping centre is small and winds along the main street, with the bowling club and the RSL clubs holding centre stage.

A supermarket, set well back from the main road, runs short of supplies when the ship from mainland Australia is unable to dock due to bad weather.

We discover secluded beaches, usually hidden from tourists, and we share them with the locals after playing golf on the gentle course bordering the seashore.

You feel both insulated and isolated here and I find it just wonderful to be so divorced from the ease and excess of Australia.

I notice a hairdresser tucked away among the small businesses lining the main street, and decide to investigate. I am welcomed

by Tiffany. She is an Islander, recently returned to Norfolk after spending six years in Brisbane. Her family, originally from Italy, have lived in Norfolk for three generations. Tiffany is working three jobs, loving the variety and relishing the opportunity to live at home and save money to buy her own place on the island.

'The pandemic has changed life,' she says.

Many of her friends are also returning to Norfolk Island to live their lives.

'Oh, it's so wonderful to be horseriding again, to play netball and touch football, all within about twenty minutes driving time,' she says. 'And the best thing of all is to be with my friends again. I don't miss the big city at all, and even though family ties can be too close for comfort, I can cope with this, and in the end just love the feeling of community and belonging.'

It is Christmas. Tiffany is planning traditional Islander celebrations, where teams of New Zealanders wearing black, Islanders wearing white, Australians wearing yellow, and Pacific Islanders wearing green get together to compete in games and contests against each other.

'It's the one time that we can all get together as Norfolk Islanders, and it's such great fun,' she says.

In pandemic-weary Australia, it is such a breath of fresh air to experience life on this Pacific Island, a simplified slower life, close to nature and to the sea.

We are reluctant to return home.

A Christian Orthodox cathedral in Kyiv, Ukraine

Wakefield Press is an independent publishing and
distribution company based in Adelaide, South Australia.
We love good stories and publish beautiful books.
To see our full range of books, please visit our website at
www.wakefieldpress.com.au
where all titles are available for purchase.
To keep up with our latest releases, news and events,
subscribe to our monthly newsletter.

Find us!

Facebook: www.facebook.com/wakefield.press
Twitter: www.twitter.com/wakefieldpress
Instagram: www.instagram.com/wakefieldpress

Printed in Australia
AUHW012053111122
371346AU00001B/1

9 781743 059630